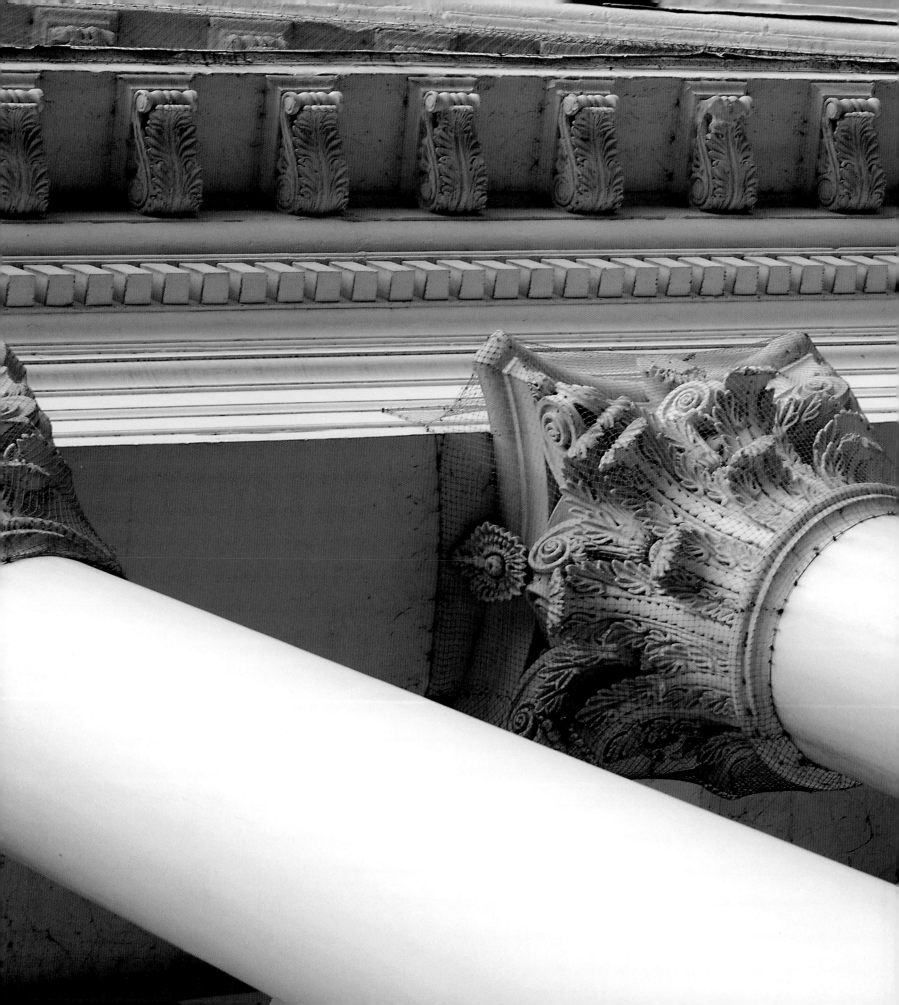

Cheltenham

Winter in Pittville Park

For Sarah, and with special thanks to Harry and Gill Potter

Cheltenham

Stephen Morris

F

FRANCES LINCOLN LIMITED

PUBLISHERS

Thanks

John Nicoll commissioned the book, thanks John.

Josie Mattock and Heidi Lawford at the Ladies' College and Natalie Whistance at Cheltenham College were exceptionally generous.

Jackie McKenzie got me into the Everyman Theatre and Ray Pearson the Masonic Lodge. Julie Sargent let me shoot pictures at the Lido on a busy summer's day. The staff at the Town Hall and at the Pump Room were great. Rachel Jones got me onto the University's Park Campus. Ian George got me a pass for the Music Festival. Joyce Cummings and John Henry gave me a steer on people and places and Claire Hickman advised on the history of English spas.

Queen's Hotel showed me the view from the roof, as did Nicola at Eagle Star Tower.

The editor and staff at *This England* magazine couldn't have been more enthusiastic in showing off Alma House. The volunteer guides at St Mary's Parish Church helped with access and history and imparted some of their love for the building. Roger Jones advised on the architecture of Lansdown and Lypiatt Terrace and pointed me in the right direction with research.

Around town, strangers let me look out from balconies and hang out of windows, and made me welcome.

Frances Lincoln Ltd
4 Torriano Mews
Torriano Avenue
London NW5 2RZ
www.franceslincoln.com

Cheltenham
Copyright © Frances Lincoln 2009
Text copyright © Stephen Morris 2009
Photographs copyright © Stephen Morris 2009
First Frances Lincoln edition: 2009

A catalogue record for this book is available from the British Library.

ISBN 978-0-7112-2903-7

Printed and bound in Singapore

9 8 7 6 5 4 3 2 1

Contents

Walking

Walking round Cheltenham on a June morning or in winter, with a weak sun poking through the mist on Leckhampton Hill, it's easy to be alone with the town. Easy too to speculate: to wonder how and why on this flat Gloucester plain, between the Cathedral at Gloucester and the Cotswold Hills, a town so fanciful – so not *country* – could ever have appeared, lying as it did by a modest stream a good three-day ride from London.

The answer, of course, is in the water. Not the green Chelt that once drove the mill wheels and now floods the High Street, but the salty water that the pigeons pecked out and the old men drank to purge their passages.

Water and timing. In Regency England whether or not one took the waters was a measure of one's social stature, how often, a measure of one's bank balance and aspirations.

Because for healthy young and not so young things water was but an aperitif. Balls, dinners, riding, flirting and pairing were the real business of any spa, and the speculators and chancers who built Cheltenham understood this perfectly well. Pittville and the Park, Montpellier and Bayshill and the shops of the Promenade are built both to attract Society and to entertain it.

A half-mad king found solace here. William Cobbett loathed it – despised the grand merry-go-round upon which he was never invited to ride. Sons and daughters of the Empire found Cheltenham's climate, its gentility and cheap lodgings to their liking and retired here.

Today, though knocked about by twentieth-century speculators and penny-pinching builders, the town remains a wonder of elegance and function. The workers' terraces in Fairview, the flats of Lansdown Terrace and the villas on the Park, the Lido, the bandstands, the spies of GCHQ, the students and the summer festivals – Cheltenham is proof that a lovely town can also be a working one.

Lansdown Terrace

Obscurity

Before the Spa there was the Street: Cheltenham Street some people said or Cheltenham: *chelt* a Saxon word for height or cliff and *ham* meaning settlement. Today, standing on Leckhampton Hill and looking west across the flat lands to the Severn, you can see the modern town sprawling Gloucester-wards and absorbing villages round-abouts. Below the Hill lies the village-cum-suburb of Charlton Kings where, long before Domesday, a chapel stood – its priest fetched from the mother church in Cheltenham.

From time to time builders in the town dig up bits of pottery and primitive weapons and, in 1916, near the now demolished Plough on the High Street, men digging a drain uncovered a bounty of Roman coins. In 2002 archeologists found evidence at Arle of seasonal occupation in the Late Iron Age, that long stretch of time before Caesar arrived from Gaul.

But that's all. Pre-historic man buried his dead at Belas Knapp and happily left his mark up here on Leck-hampton Hill – anywhere in fact where the slope of the land made him feel safe in life and special in death. Yet in the vale he has left only a handful of tools and bits of pottery to mark his passing. It's understandable; who, after all, would risk it down there?

The Romans and their mercenary armies would. To the Romans, Britain was a fabled but obscure island protected by a sea of fearsome tides. Invasion was an act of imperial bravura and yet, in two short campaigns, Caesar conquered the tribes and absorbed them into the Empire.

The Romans built villas at Winchcombe, Witcombe, Whittington, Withington and Chedworth and a fortress at Cirencester. Corinium became the second city of Roman Britain, at the hub of the Empire's road network and garrisoned by the Legio XX – 12,000 people living under its protection. But Cheltenham? The legions of Britannia Prima might have marched this way and dropped their coins here, but no Roman settlement ever took root by the Chelt.

In fact, we first hear of Cheltenham long after the Romans have gone, in a Britain subdued by the 'red and savage tongue' of Saxon and Angle invaders (the Saxons took Gloucester in 577) and, from early in the seventh century, shaped by Augustine's Christian church.

Around 770 King Offa ruled Mercia, issued beautiful coins and built a dyke to keep out the Welsh. And at that time a 'monastery' was built somewhere here. For 30 years the monastery (or whatever it was) paid revenues to the see of Worcester until, in 803, the Bishop of Hereford claimed the money as his own. The two bishops settled their dispute at the Council of Cloveshoe where *Cheltenham* in Mercia entered written history.

Between Cloveshoe and Domesday in 1086 the monastery was lost. Perhaps it was never much of a building but more a gathering of priests like a parish, or maybe it was destroyed by the Danes who, after sacking Gloucester in 877, pursued their blood lust further east. And like its monastery Cheltenham was lost too – or at least fell quiet. Not until Domesday does it reappear, as *Terra Regis*, with an account of land and ploughs and grinding mills. According to the *Anglo-Saxon Chronicle*, in 1085 William I was at Gloucester when the Domesday Survey was agreed and this is feasible: Gloucester was a royal fortress where William held court each mid-winter; a garrison to counter wild Welsh ambitions.

On Leckhampton Hill
Up here, when imagination feels the footfall of Iron Age man, Cheltenham is a reassuring presence.

In 1086, William's Domesday commissioners arrived in the hundred – the local measure of justice – to question the sheriffs, barons and freemen and to find out who and what was here. In the original Latin, Domesday says that 'Chinteneha' comprised a manor with 24 plough teams, five mills and 114 tenants. The church held some land and the *terra regis* (and this is what William really wanted to know) yearly paid the crown £20, 20 cows and 20 hogs. The hundred measured five by six miles – you could have walked it in a day – and was centred on the modern town where the manor

house stood – somewhere near the modern High Street. Lord's Meadow, identified in Domesday, survived as farm land until the early-nineteenth century when it became the Promenade.

Here, in 1100, life is ticked off by the seasons. There is a church, mills and a manor house, and common fields in which history occasionally leaves a footprint. In 1135, for example, when the death of Henry I (from eating too many eels) precipitated a dynastic struggle between his daughter Matilda and nephew Stephen. In the ensuing anarchy Matilda made Gloucester her powerbase and for four years Welsh and Flemish mercenaries, like the Danes before them, mauraded through the hundred giving Cheltenham's farmers cause to resent and fear their big city neighbour. At Postlip under Cleeve Hill the lovely Norman church of St James commemorates the murder by soldiers of worshippers on their way to church in Winchcombe.

Henry II restored order to England and in 1221 his son, Henry III – the great legislator – sent six justices to Gloucester to enforce royal justice. The court records of their sitting (another of Henry's innovations) give a first glimpse of real Cheltonians and, frankly, it doesn't flatter. Hugo and Matilda and their two children John and Julia, are murdered in their home; the murderer escapes and is never caught. A travelling merchant with 15 marks in his pocket lodges in the house of Agnes and her son Alexander. Neither merchant nor his money are ever seen again. John of Brockhampton murders Christine of Arle and (unsuccessfully) seeks sanctuary of the church.

At the same time and with a bloodlust ill-suited to his office, Giles de Braose, Bishop of Hereford, built a gallows on common pasture at Prestbury near the racecourse. And yet few criminals were caught and, poor bishop, fewer hanged but order was maintained and in the medieval way of things Cheltenham prospered. It may have been a long and terrible road to London (the figures in the church were of Christopher and Erasmus – patron saints of travellers) but the climate was kind and the soil exceptionally rich: a black and red loam in which carrots, cabbages, oats, leeks and turnips grew and on which after harvest, Gloucester cattle grazed.

At Sunday service in St Mary's the medieval farmer, hands clasped fervently in prayer, might seek devine deliverance from plague, sickness and anarchy. And if his payers were answered and the apocalypse postponed, outside in the spring sunshine there were opportunities to profit from the land he worked, to sell his produce and to prosper. But to do that, first of all he needed a market.

St James Postlip

The Norman church of St James Postlip was built by William de Solers 'moved by the tears of his tenants waylaid and plundered' at Cleeve Hill on their way to Winchcombe Church. Sit here on a summer's day or in winter when the crows caw and time stops.

Emergence

In 1226 Henry III granted Cheltenham a market 'each week on a Thursday' and a fair each year 'to last for three days'. He also leased the manor to 'the men of Cheltenham' at £64 a year for six years. In effect, Henry handed over the keys to the door. His sheriff no longer held sway: he could neither levy fines and dues nor send in bailiffs. In turn, whoever held the lease administered the hundred, regulated the market and whooped it up at the fair. It wasn't democratic, but it was the beginnings of the borough.

And then love or lust intervened. In 1232 Henry gave Cheltenham to his gorgeous bride, Eleanor of Province, as part of her dower. The 12-year-old beauty stormed the English court and, with a retinue of posturing Savoyard cousins, drove a dangerous wedge between the King and his barons. Worse, on her death in 1291 Cheltenham passed to the Abbey de Fécamp on the Normandy coast in exchange for Rye and Winchelsea – ports the Abbey had held after cutting a deal with Cnut.

Thus began foreign monastic ownership on terms so generous that it became the 'Liberty of Cheltenham' – a manor with all royal liberties to raise money, enforce customs and distribute justice. And of course in reality and not withour precendent, the abbots of Fécamp feathered their beds as best they could according to how their authority ebbed and flowed with the fortunes of the Hundred Years War. In 1410 Henry IV torched Fécamp and on the eve of Agincourt in 1415, Henry V finally redeemed all foreign ownership of manors for the English crown. He conferred the manor of Cheltenham on his aunt Elizabeth and her husband John Cornwall, who was one of Henry's

'happy few' at Agincourt and made a bagful of money ransoming Louis Bourbon, who he captured in battle.

By now Cheltenham was a community of carpenters, bakers, brewers, millers and farmers, perhaps 350 tenants, their families and labourers. Tenants paid dues to the manor – for selling a horse, for a marriage licence and a penny for pannage (the right to feed pigs) in the woods – and of course, they paid rent. Matilda Bayse paid 9s. a year for 60 acres and delivered letters for the lord of the manor. Her name survives in Bayshill.

Labour service by tenant to lord – delivering letters, plowing or tilling – was all but lost after the Great Mortality of 1349, when those tenants who remained alive paid money, work silver, instead. Spreading from Devon, the Great Mortality – the Black Death as it became – reached and wasted Bristol. Terrified, the 'men of Gloucester refused those of Bristol entrance to their county.' In vain. In Gloucestershire, as in England, thousands fell. The young and strong died first; the graveyards overflowed with the unburied dead.

In a population of maybe four million, one in three died, so that at the end of 1349 a healthy body was a rare and valuble commodity and only a fool would sell his body cheaply. While fields fell fallow and villages vanished the old chains of labour service weakened. Two hundred years would pass before England replenished its lost population but meanwhile, if you were still alive, it wasn't a bad time to be a peasant.

Wages rose and rents fell. In Cheltenham, the tenants and tradesmen knew what they were worth and it was more than a beleaguered state would tolerate. In 1422, two special court sessions met at the

St Mary's, the parish church
The glass rose or wheel window, sometimes called St Catherine's, has an elementary error in its composition.
Six hundred years ago an earthquake damaged the church. Zealots stole from it and whitewashed the walls. In 1879,
the rector tried to close it. Inside there is peace and a warm beauty in the stones. St Mary's is a survivor.

manor house, probably on the site now occupied by St Matthew's Church, to 'curb the malice of servants who were idle and not willing to serve after the pestilence without excessive wages.'

The court record from 1422 is unequivocal: everyone was on the make. Nine weavers were fined for charging 6*d*. above the 'proper' wage. Bakers, butchers, ostlers, farmers, thatchers, fishermen, tanners and maltsters – all took a turn in front of the justices and

were fined for profiteering – no doubt putting up their prices to pay the fine. Like Chaucer's streetwise pilgrims they lived in a time of opportunity and took every opportunity to prosper. Woodcutters on 1*s*. 8*d*. a day demanded more money to buy ale when the sun shone and the work was harder.

The manor was once more in monastic ownership, the gift of a war-weary and grateful Henry V to his new monastery of Syon on the Thames by Teddington. The monastery leased the land and employed two stewards and a bailiff to collect the rent. It wasn't easy. In a de-populated, post-plague world the tenants were not going to be told how much to pay. The bailiff called for help from Lord Sudeley and 46 horsemen were sent to negotiate but even so, the tenants won.

By 1500 Cheltenham had a manor house and modest timber-framed houses on a single street with a market place. There were grand houses at Arle and Leckhampton. In the fields tenant farmers worked side-by-side in open strips and after harvest, grazed their animals in common pasture. There was a simple bridge and stepping stones across the Chelt to reach the church and a road for carts to Gloucester.

Today, only St Mary's survives. To see Cheltenham through the eyes of sixteenth-century man you have to slip through the alley by The Famous outfitters on the High Street ('always look after the man who wants to buy a collar stud; he may want a shirt some day') and into the parish church.

St Mary's is the oldest building here by 600 years. An earlier church was endowed by Reinbald who was later canon at Cirencester Abbey. We will never know what vision occured to Reinbald that he should build a church here but after his death the Abbey built St Mary's in the same spot. By 1500, the parish church was already old. The west wall and the piers and arches of the west tower are Norman. The lower part of the tower is early English and the spire is four-teenth century. In 1509 Richard Machyn gifted £6 to build the middle aisle and William Greville of Arle Court endowed 25s. p.a. for bread for the poor. There were shrines to Saints Christopher and Erasmus and, from 1500, two chantries – endowments to pay for priests to pray every day for the founders and for all Christian souls.

By 1550, boys were learning Latin and Greek in the north aisle. One of them may have been Richard Pate who later gave his name to the town's first grammar school. Elizabeth I granted Pate the chantry money taken by her father at Dissolution 'for the exercise of grammar and other liberal arts and science' and in 1574 on the High Street the Schola Gramatica admitted its first boys at 4d. each. At the same time Pate's Almshouses opened.

Today and most days at St Mary's there is a 15-minute lunchtime service in the chapel. It is a beautiful place and peaceful, but this is England and so peace is a conceit: like every other early church in England, St Mary's has known violence and betrayal, schism and hatred.

At Dissolution, Bishop Hooper – one of Henry VIII's stormtroopers – destroyed the shrines and screens. Money bequethed to the chantries and even bread money for the poor was confiscated for the crown. The chantry priests, Grove and Ball, were sacked and from 1554 the service was delivered in English – and only English. The curate Stephen Poole (such an ordinary name to be caught in great events) was tested for his command of the 'new' Christian faith and shortly after disappears from view.

After a short and bloody counter-reformation under Mary (who burned the Bishop of Gloucester, John Hooper, for 'generously refusing the Queen's pardon') Elizabeth I brutally enforced her supremacy. As for Westminster Abbey so for St Mary's: in Eliza-beth's time heads were counted at church and absen-tees noted; only papists and Puritans missed the serv-ice and some were hanged for it. In Cheltenham, by faith or common sense the congregation took communion in the Elizabethan way.

Besides, the community had other things to think about. War with Spain coupled with Elizabeth's reluc-tance to collect taxes – she preferred to sell monopo-lies and honours – had ravaged the economy; the enclosure of common fields and rising unemployment created a body of transient poor some of whom, horror of horrors, were carrying plague. For ten years until 1600 there were four burials for every baptism at St Mary's font. Ten years later, the horrors were still fresh when a group of players turned up to perform at the Crown. Guy Dobbins marched down the street banging a drum to draw a crowd. The bailiff apprehended him, fined him and sent the company packing down the terrible road to Gloucester.

Plague aside, in 1600 the able-bodied were profiting nicely from the fertile soil by the Chelt. *Men and Armour* (1608) says there were 350 men fit to fight: 130 of them worked on the land and there were cobblers, tailors and maltsters. There were eels and trout in the brook, plenty of barley for beer and the beginnings of a tobacco crop. The old Booth Hall had been made into a second market house. There were at least two inns, the Crown and the Plough; the Plough survived on the site of the Regents Arcade until 1982.

Above Arcadia floated a few clouds: Puritans for example, who stopped maypoles and dancing and ales on saints' days (except in Charlton Kings). The old manorial knots were slipping and in 1625 the Cheltenham Act changed how land was held and inherited (and gave a widow rights to one third of their husband's holdings). Now, families whose names came to shape the community – Packer and Gough, Norwood and Pate, Ashmead, Machin and Gregory – appeared as freeholders able to pass on their inheritence and create – god-willing – a stable and dynastic community.

Stable, but not necessarily law-abiding and certainly dynamic. John Norwood knew Walter Raleigh and Raleigh brought tobacco back from Virginia. Norwood himself may have brought it to Cheltenham but in any event, Cheltenham's farmers were quick to plant it in the rich loam.

James I loathed smoking but rather than ban tobacco, he allowed imports of it from the colonies and in 1619 made home-grown crops illegal. He was whistling in the wind. Eight years later, Charles I ordered Gloucestershire growers to appear before the Privy Council; at Winchcombe his writ was ritually shredded. Oliver Cromwell sent a battle-hardened troop of horse under Cornet Joyce to destroy the crop at Cheltenham but they were repelled by 'an armed multitude guarding the tobacco field.' (Bizarrely, Joyce was later accused by Charles II's astrologer of being his father's masked executioner and fearing for his life after the Restoration fled to Holland). Charles II ordered all tobacco plants to be uprooted but when the sheriff turned out to enforce the order, Cheltenham growers threatened a riot and the sheriff and his men retreated. Ultimately, cheap tobacco from Virginia and a price crash spoiled a once-profitable business, and the farmers replaced tobacco with barley.

Armed bands were never welcome. In 1643 Gloucester, the troublesome neighbour, was besieged by Charles I – stubborn, bloody-minded Charles who, in marching on Gloucester missed his chance to take London. Instead, he gave Parliament breathing space and, incredibly, Parliament used it to raise 15,000 men under Essex.

On 4 September 1643 the parliamentary army reached Cleeve Hill where, in foul weather, their artillery fired a fusilade of warning shots across the vale. Next day the infantry, drenched and angry and trampling the crops, advanced through Prestbury and Southam and engaged with a royalist vanguard by the Chelt. Enough. Charles fled to Gloucester. The victors free quartered at Cheltenham for three days where some found solace at St Mary's (and whitewashed the once decorative walls) and others in the local ale.

The civil war was a time of shifing loyalties when politics changed with bewildering speed. At outbreak the local MP and owner of the manor, John 'Crump' Dutton, backed Charles I but later refused the King money and when his daughter Lucy gave Charles shelter at Cobberley, Dutton cut off her inheritance. Instead he favoured his nephew Will Dutton and made Oliver Cromwell guardian to the boy. Will spent two years in Cromwell's household where he was tutored by the poet Andrew Marvell, a master of equivocation who taught Will how to survive and taught him well.

**Tudor fireplace
de la Bere Hall,
Southam**
Built by John
Huddleston whose wife
Joan was aunt to Jane
Seymour, Henry VIII's
third bride.
The de la Bere family
served the manor of
Cheltenham for
generations. George III
popped in during his
Cheltenham stay.
In 1841 Lord
Ellenborough,
Governor-General of
India, bought it.

In 1667, after the Restoration, Charles II appointed William sheriff of Cheltenham.

Gloucester and Winchcombe were both destroyed but with neither a castle to raze nor strategic value, Cheltenham survived. Shipping on the Severn was hampered by the armies but the market prospered and tobacco and barley grew abundantly. Retribution, especially religious retribution, fell on the town after Restoration.

In 1662 Charles II's Act of Uniformity restored the rites and ceremonies of the old church that existed before Cromwell and the Puritans brushed them away with the bishops. John Cooper, the curate at St Mary's and 'an able preaching minister,' was sacked. The town's Quakers went underground and 15 of them, including Richard Wall and Tobias Leech, left for America where, on land belonging to William Penn, they created a new Cheltenham in Pennsylvania. Back home Elizabeth Sandford was imprisoned and beaten 'in the flesh oft times severely' and other Friends were tried and fined for worshipping. It would not last.

A protestant Prince William of Orange and the Glorious Revolution conferred (unless you were a Catholic) a new tolerance on a country riven by faith. Quakers, Baptists and Presbyterians came out of the cupboard and in Cheltenham there was William Mason, a Quaker and hosier of Bays Hill who, with a little bit of luck and a son-in-law, was about to change the future of the town.

Water

By 1700 Cheltenham Street was half a mile long. There were buildings on both sides: Pate's Grammar School and Almshouses, malthouses and mills, three pubs: the Plough, the Crown and the Fleece, two market houses, the manor and, just off the street, the Blind House (a small stone-built prison) and punishment stocks for miscreants. There were four crossings of the Chelt to join the street with the church and church house: two simple bridges and two lines of stepping stones. To the north there was common pasture on the marshy land towards Pittville and St Paul's. With the end of tobacco, the fields were planted with barley and, save for Sundays when malting was forbidden, the smell of malt and malthouses pervaded. More than 1,500 people lived here in 300 houses: millers and farmers, carpenters and builders, clothiers and tailors, maltsters and brewers. There was a market every thursday and a fair on St James's Day (25 July). The turnpike was yet to reach the town and there was no direct coach service to London which, at three to five miles an hour, was still three days away.

In 1718 in a field on Bays Hill about half a mile from the parish church (and now the site of Princess Hall in the Ladies' College) William Mason put a fence around a spring of water on his land.

Mason knew the tales of pigeons pecking at the salt deposited by the water and of old men drinking it to purge their ailments. He knew about the Hotwells spring in Bristol (his son Joseph lived there) and about the spas at Harrogate, Epsom and Tunbridge Wells. There were drinking spas everywhere. The English loved their water and the holy well, once pagan, then Christian and later Popish, was now dressed up in science and reason. Doctors prescribed mineral water for a thousand ailments and patients – faced with blood-letting, purging and other ghastly remedies – drank it.

Mason put a shed around his spring on Bays Hill and locked the door. Even Bath Spa was struggling to turn a good profit so why risk money making Cheltenham pay? Besides, the road was awful, there was nowhere to stay and nothing to do.

But Mason was curious and hired two doctors to find out what was in the water. Predictably they found a mild chalybeate, a compound of mineral salts and iron (it's the iron that gives chalybeate its characteristic taste) favoured by physicians of the day. The star of English medicine and 'chemical doctor' par excellence, Thomas Sydenham, prescribed chalybeate as an antidote to hysteria, ague, fatique and most other ailments.

In 1720, Mason ran advertisements in the *Gloucester Journal* (and later in the London press) extolling the curative qualities of his springwater, the 'convenient lodgings' in the town, its fine bowling green and billiard tables.

> These waters youth in age renew
> Strength to the weak and sickly add
> Give the pale cheek a rosy hue
> And cheerful spirits to the sad.

Even modest claims were deceitful. The Plough was 'convenient' (and had 42 bedrooms), but would a gentleman stay there with his family and let them watch bear-baiting from the bedroom window? Few would, few did.

Pittville Pump Room
This strange time-traveller machine dispenses water to bemused visitors who taste it and screw their faces up.
Come and find the tap but remember:
'Tis neccesary to quicken your motions after a second glass'.

Like Bath and Hotwells, if Cheltenham was going to attract visitors then it needed lodgings, amusements and intelligent diversions; it needed investors with money and vision. Possessed of neither, Mason let the land for £61 a year and retired to Bristol.

Spa

In St Mary's there is a memorial to Captain Henry Skillicorne; with a chair to sit on it's possible to read it all. It is probably the longest obituary ever written in stone: a flunkied but helpful description of him: 'tall, erect, robust, active' who 'lived and died an honest man'.

Skillicorne was a Manxman and a gentleman seafarer living in Bristol when, in 1731, he met and married William Mason's daughter Elizabeth. Elizabeth had inherited the Bays Hill land and in 1738, she and Henry went to live there.

That summer Henry built a fancy well-house with arches and a dome. He installed a pump disguised as an obelisk and built a room for billiards and dancing and protection in wet weather. The next year, with the help of his raffish young friend Norbonne Berkeley, he began the Old Well Walk and the Upper Walk. A year later he planted 96 elms to create the Lower Walk, an arrow straight promenade to the spire of St Mary's over Jemmy's bridge and to the church. Landscaping was expensive (the elms alone were £56) but essential to Henry's vision of Cheltenham as a pastoral playground, a concocted bit of countryside offering not just fresh air and good water but balls, billiards and intrigue. To underwrite the work he sold seasonal subscriptions with the fervour of the timeshare salesman, netting 655 subscribers who each paid 2s. for a season's water.

Water, wells, accommodation and amusements: the development of a successful English spa town followed a familiar path. A visiting duke and a hatful of lords were good for business. A favourable account by a well-known balneologist could make or break a smaller resort and, in a voguish and competitive marketplace, entrepreneurs shamelessly publicised scientific reports of their waters' curative powers.

So Dr Short's *History of Mineral Waters*, published in 1740, was a gift for Skillicorne. Short, who claimed to have analysed all the English mineral waters, declared Bays Hill chalybeate the best. The London press ran the story and declared Cheltenham *the* place to be. The mineralogist Hieronymus Senckenburg writing in *Philosophical Transactions* said he couldn't find any iron in the water, but what did he know? Cheltenham MC and dandy-in-chief Simon Moreau later declared Senckenburg's tests flawed because they were performed in London when the iron had already dissipated. To cover his tail, Moreau advised visitors to drink from a small glass rather than a big one, for fear the iron be lost in an instant.

Details details. Once the fashionistas decided Dr Short was right and Cheltenham water was good for them, only death by poisoning would stop them drinking it. As Horace Walpole said, 'People go to these places well and return cured.' Never mind the water, the visitors wanted to know where they would sleep (and who with), how they would dine and when they would dance.

As a market town Cheltenham was used to visitors and by 1750 there were three inns – the Plough, George and Crown – and another, the Swan, nearly ready. For superior types there was Lady Stapleton's Great House near the church and several improvised lodgings. The Great House became a lodging and a social hub with balls and concerts and, as visitors increased, two malthouses were turned into theatres.

Jane Edwards was a pioneer visitor who came from Bristol in the summer season of 1742 and stayed at

Fauconberg House, St George's Road
This is the 1847 version, not George III's residence.

Ketheway's, where she paid £7 10*s*. for five weeks. As was the way, Ms Edwards rented several rooms and brought a maid, possibly a cook, a ton of coal, honey and beer. Provisions, especially coal, were critical to spa growth and in 1792 Cheltenham would cut a canal from the Severn to carry supplies to town. Meanwhile, Jane Edwards brought coal with her or paid a 'serious sum' locally for it. She paid 2*s*. to drink the water at Skillicorne's well and whined to her diary about the price of a sedan chair (10*s*. 6*d*. a week). She gave 7*s*. 6*d*. to the bell ringers who rang her into town.

As a keen spa-goer Jane Edwards would have noted how, unlike Bath, Cheltenham was neither confined by hills nor troubled by narrow and crowded streets and that beyond the street lay unenclosed common land. She'd also have noted the men who farmed the land:

St George's Road
Young trees grow green
in a stuccoed garden.

robust, cock-fighting, footballing ruffians who nightly gathered on the street and who were (thank goodness) excluded from the Walks. The young pretender to Bath's polite society still had a lot to learn. However, the attractions of a new spa and one with miraculous waters was enough to tempt the wealthy and the sick.

In 1743 the *Morning Post* reported 600 summer visitors: a company of 'fortune and gentility' including at the apex, the commander of the British Army, John Campbell, Duke of Argyll (who thrashed the Jacobites at Sheriffmuir in 1715) and his wife the Duchess. Unfortunately, the Duke died a couple of months after taking the cure, in October 1743.

Visitors of calibre attracted a train of suppliers, craftsmen and labourers, investors and entrepreneurs. Thomas Pope bought the Plough and the Great House (where he staged assemblies, balls and concerts) and improvised a theatre in an old malthouse. The Irish impresario John Watson brought Sarah Siddons to play *High Life Below Stairs*. Watson later built a new little theatre at Cambray where Siddons, the darling of the English stage, played to her public for 40 guineas a night – serious money that pumped up the price of a seat. (In 1807 she returned to the Cambray to play Lady Macbeth – the leitmotif of a glittering career).

A Monmouth-born lawyer, Thomas Hughes, who first came to Cheltenham as clerk to John de la Bere, rented the Old Well from an ageing Skillicorne and around 1750 began bottling the water under the 'Spaw' label. Hughes married well and used his wife's money to buy land and an ageing ballroom on the High Street.

A London man with an eye for a deal, William Miller, went into business with Skillicorne's son William (who had inherited his father's estate) and pumped money into the Bays Hill site. In 1776 the pair opened the Long Room at Bays Hill to provide a new and bigger space for balls and dining. Almost before the paint was dry, Thomas Hughes announced plans for a new and (if you believed him) long-planned Assembly Rooms nearby: a fabulous new venue that would attract the cream of the company. A feud ensued between Miller and Hughes fed by handbills and accusations in the letters page of the *Morning Post*. Miller, who must have had some influence over the editor, was credited with taking a village spa, one that was blindly hanging on to its rural obscurity, and making it into a place 'at least sufferable' by high-income, big-spending visitors.

In reality, both Miller and Hughes were going to make money. Both their ventures were largely funded by subscription with little capital risk, an unstable Europe made British tourists look closer to home for their pleasures and turnpike mania, the fit of roadbuilding that was sweeping the country in the 1770s, meant the little spa, a 'happy mixture of London elegance and rural delight,' was now only 26 hours from Mayfair.

During the season of April to October, Miller's Long Room was open for breakfast every morning when 200 to 300 people sat down to eat. There was a ball every Monday. Hughes's Assembly Rooms had card parties on a Thursday and Friday and Miller and Hughes had sense enough to take turns on a Thursday ball. There was theatre at least twice a week.

The aristocracy came mostly for pleasure but Lord Fauconberg came to treat his scurvy (one of many ailments that the water was claimed to cure) and stayed, commissioning William Skillicorne to build Fauconberg House for him.

The Assembly Rooms – which had more bling than was tasteful – thrust their newness into the 'coarse old buildings' of the old High Street: the Corn Market, Butter Cross and lock-up. Propelled by business interests the old buildings were flattened. The High Street was 'neatly flagged and paved' and oil lights were installed to light the way for evening promenaders. The Chelt, a rambling brook that powered the mill at Cambray and was occassionally diverted to wash the waste off the old street, was cut and channelled. Business was good for the town and business – thanks to one special and unforseen visitor – was about to go mad.

Madness

Poor, mad porphyriac George, Farmer George who smelt of horses. His eldest son was a freespending dandy and his prime minister a runt who fiddled when America burned. In 28 troubled years George had travelled only to Oxford and Portsmouth and knew nothing of the land he ruled.

In June 1788, after a 'pretty smart billious attack' the lord of the bedchamber Lord Fauconberg suggested the King might try Cheltenham water and stay at Fauconberg House, his modest but comfortable home in Bays Hill. George Baker, the King's increasingly desperate physician, agreed.

In July 1788 the circus rolled into town and occupied Fauconberg House (now demolished). Bizarrely, when George's second son, Frederick Duke of York, came to join the party he lodged at a portable wooden house that was moved along the High Street inch-by-inch so that father and son could be near one another.

It's hard to think of George III and not think of Nigel Hawthorne. Alan Bennett's eccentric, simple Mr King in *The Madness of King George* is the man who for five weeks made Cheltenham the centre of the fashionable world. At six every morning the royal party, George, Charlotte and the three princesses, drank from the Old Well. A contemporary cartoon depicts an engorged king drinking voraciously but in fact the water supply was modest and to meet demand the King sank a new well 12 foot from the old one. It was called the King's Well. The King's pumper was Hannah Forty, a gardener's wife who pumped for 43 years and is buried in St Mary's.

After taking the water George filled his days walking and riding. He called on the de la Beres in Southam and rode up Cleeve Hill to examine the earth works in an obsessive, nose-to-the-ground kind of way. He called for bats and balls and watched his idling servants play cricket, and sat at the window of Fauconberg House tending to affairs of state. Come September when parliament returned, the Whigs would force a debate on the King's fitness to serve but for now, in a sweet summer of lucidity, the business of state was his and his alone – however much the Prince of Wales might want the seal of state.

The King walked without a retinue or bodyguard and sometimes rode alone in farmer's clothes, eyeing the Gloucester cattle and talking prices with the farmers so that, unwittingly, George, King of Hanover, became as English as the English themselves, and Cheltenham liked him for it.

The royal party dined at five and in the evening promenaded on the Well Walk and the High Street (now 'extremely long, clean and well-paved') attracting a swarm of curious on-lookers.

The party went to Worcester to hear Handel at the Three Choirs Festival and to Tewkesbury to see the abbey. On Sundays they prayed at St Mary's where the choir couldn't sing for nerves and where a bassoon was found to accompany the hymns.

In August a party came from Bath and begged the King to visit Bath instead, but Cheltenham suited George. He liked the simplicity of the town; he liked walking his little dogs through the orchards and riding the breeze in the upland meadows; he liked the hills and the farms and Watson's cramped theatre where the lovely Dorothea Bland, 'Mrs Jordan', played in *She Would and She Would Not*. (She certainly would and later did, as mistress to George's third son William IV).

John Dower House
Originally called the Clarence Hotel after the visit of the Duchess of Clarence, later Queen Adelaide wife of William IV. She was not William's first choice and William already had ten children by actress 'Mrs Jordan', who he saw play at Watson's Cambray Theatre. He wrote 'She is doomed, poor dear innocent young creature, to be my wife.'

For five weeks that summer the King was sane and Cheltenham was the centre of the universe.

When the Majestic spirit of the law
Feels a relief from Cheltenham's humble spa;
When George, our Constitution's sacred shield,
Here, aids his own, the Sceptre long to wield.

Cheltenham fashion as modelled by pretty young things at the Well Walk and in the ballrooms, was the business. 'The Cheltenham cap, the Cheltenham bonnet, the Cheltenham buttons, the Cheltenham buckles – all fashions are completely Cheltenhamised' said London's *Morning Post. Gentleman's Quarterly*, before reporting ecclesiastical preferments and parliamentary proceedings, told its readers what the King and Queen had had for breakfast (jam and fruit). The watercolourist Peter La Cave came to town and sketched the royal party at the well and on the Well Walk – sellable subjects and ideally suited to La Cave's 'picturesque' style.

As well as the royal party there were 1,500 in the company that summer, including four earls, six lords and the Bishop of Gloucester, who couldn't keep away and gave the services at St Mary's. The lodgings were full and the inns overflowed. Late-comers found rooms in Prestbury and Teweksbury.

Who knows how the King found peace here, but for a short while he did and the regal sanity returned. It was a sweet but brief respite, a temporary cure and a prequel to a sorry story that began with a band on the High Street playing 'God save the King' as the royal party left for London and finished 32 years later, with a deaf, blind, mad – and dead – Farmer George.

By contrast, Cheltenham's star ascended. After a blip for the French Revolution and recession, when visitors fell by half, the town boomed. Daniel Freeman opened warm baths, lodgings went up and luxury tradesmen – silver and goldsmiths, milliners and wig-makers – came up from London. The printer and bookseller Samuel Harward built Harward's Buildings (the municipal offices on the Promenade). Even now their monumental symmetry is breathtaking. There were two banks to keep the money moving and two breweries, including Gardner's Ale and Porter Brewery.

By 1796 there was a population of 3,000 and a seasonable company of 1,600. One visitor that summer, Joshua Gilpin, a rich paper merchant from Philadelphia, complained to his diary about the awful lodgings and outrageous prices: rooms at two guineas a week (plus 18s. for the maid and cook) and dances more than a £1. Even the King's old pumper, Mrs Forty, was charging 5s. to draw the water.

Gilpin was caught in a seller's market. England was at war with France, Holland and Spain. Continental spas were closed to English tourists and the coast was unsafe. Food was short, work was scarce and the bigger towns and cities were at tipping point; the wealthy looked closer to home for amusement. And when Bath was overcrowded and *so* yesterday, where better to go than Cheltenham – where widows find their husbands over whist and 'the water is less windy'?

As the continental war pushed the economy towards financial meltdown Bath, with its huge investments and infrastructure, faced bankruptcy and starvation and the Bath mob, which had frightened away visitors in the 1780s, was back on the streets. At Clifton Hotwells building work stopped for ten years; the spa never recovered.

'We pity a lamb dragged to the slaughter house' wrote Humphrey Ruff in his 1803 guide, 'how much more is our pity when we contemplate the sacrifice of youth at Bristol Hotwells.' He could afford to be smug: Cheltenham was going to have a very good war.

Under pressure from business interests, in 1801 the Enclosure Act finally freed land from common use so that parcels could be sold as building plots.

As Napoleon threatened half of Europe, as banks crashed and prices rose, when work was hard to find, John Watson bought most of Cambray. He built a new theatre – the Theater Royal – and found a chalybeate spring where he built a pump and opened the Cambray Spa in 1802. It was the first challenge to Skillicorne's Old Well which was now running slowly and soon would be used only by servants.

Joseph Pitt, a Cirencester lawyer who began business holding horses for a penny, bought 250 acres of land including the Marsh to the north of the High Street. Here he planned Pittville, his dream town. Lord Sherbourne, as lord of the manor with a nice flow of dues, queered Pitt's ambitions for 20 years but Pitt had patience: Pittville would come. Meanwhile, in shameless imitation of Bath he built the Royal Crescent, the first of the grand terraces.

In 1801, Henry Thompson, a 'chattering box' Liverpudlian, bought 400 acres from the de la Beres in Montpellier and Lansdown and began digging for mineral water. He took 80 borings. At the same time Dr Jameson made 40 holes in Imperial Square.

Thompson found water in Montpellier in 1808 and there he built a pump room with walks and rides. The avenues created later became Montpellier Spa Road, Montpellier Parade, Terrace, Villa and Grove. Thompson also built a house for himself (now Vittoria House in Vittoria Walk) and in 1809 he built baths to rival Freeman's. Patrons could bathe only in tepid or cold water but Thompson claimed 100 customers a week and Humphrey Ruff's *Cheltenham Chronicle*, a shamelessly pro-Thompson paper, declared Cheltenham a bathing spa. The present-day building and rotunda in Montpellier Walk replaced Thompson's first pump room around 1820.

Jameson's borings resulted in the Sherbourne Spa on the site of the Queen's Hotel. This soon ran dry and was replaced by the Imperial Spa in 1818. In 1810 at Alstone, a Mr Smith found a source of salty and bitter mineral water in his garden. Like everyone else, Smith opened a spa.

To compete with the new borings, Skillicorne's Old Well at which, horror, servants and trades now drank, was revamped and by 1820 offered no fewer than five types of water and salt. It was a short reprise. By 1837 when the old spring was dead and half-forgotten, the Skillicornes sold Bayshill to speculative builders. Their development of the site was crippled by one financial crisis after another but over time the terraces took shape: Royal Well Terrace, Bayshill Terrace and Queen's Parade, which was only finished in the 1980s.

In Fairview, St Pauls and St Peters there were houses for artisans and workers and all over town there were new lodging houses, stables and amenities. Bricks were made on site using the rich blue clay and cream-coloured freestone was carried from Leckhampton quarry by Charles Trye's horsedrawn tramway that had opened in 1809 with a band and a dinner for 50 at the Plough. Trye's tramway joined another at Norwood Street to run along the High Street to the coal wharf. Here, the canal and later the railway brought coal from the Forest of Dean.

With coal in the hearth, good food on the table and with better and faster coaches, visitors might come for winter and some might settle. London, the centre of the world, the heart of empire, was a pit of madness; where else might one live that was comfortable and where the fashions, the news and the theatre were no more than a day behind the capital?

The diners that night at the Plough crossed their fingers and toasted the birth of the winter resort – and a better return on their precarious investments.

Meanwhile, an obvious truth: the town was a mess, a matrix of scaffolding, rubble and dust. The commissioners (including Watson, Thompson and Pitt) took new powers to make good the streets at public expense: laying roads and pavements and adding more lights. The stink of slaughterhouses and brewhouses was controlled by shorter working hours and a 'scavenger of the rubbish' was hired (at £150 a year) to keep the streets clean.

Transients were a burden and beggars made a nusiance of themselves in the churchyard. A poor house was built and when the homeless exceeded the number of beds they were put to work on the streets. The Cheltenham Volunteers stood by to quell disturbances and faced down a half-hearted mob which broke only door knockers in Pitt's Royal Crescent and some lamps on the High Street. Soldiers were later replaced by watchmen and in 1831, by a police force like London's 'peelers'.

Across the country prices were rising faster than wages and yet locally, life was good below stairs and in the neat terraces of Fairview. The lower classes, said Dr Jameson, are 'cleanly in their houses and persons' and living a 'robust' life in the open air, eating 'moderately of animal food and freely of home-made ale and cyder.'

Sanitation was Georgian: thunderbox and cesspit and a limited supply of clean water for washing. Effluent was carried in streams and ditches; Pittville discharged its effluent straight into Hatherley Brook. Bathing at Thompson's or Freeman's was strictly medicinal and not for tradesmen; if a bath was needed at home Daniel Freeman could deliver an 'invalid's bathtub' to the house.

In 1809 the first free hospital, the Dispensary, opened and the poor – with the 'smallpox at their heels' – swamped Edward Jenner's weekly surgery for a shot of the doctor's cowpox. Jenner's revolutionary idea about 'vaccination' was a gift for the satirical cartoonists but his patients fought each other for a jab.

In 1812, 400 visitors came for the winter season and 5,000 for the summer. Lord Byron was one – 'absurd, amiable, perplexing, dangerous' Byron – who had an affair with an opera singer here and was turned down by Anne Milbanke, whose aunt, Lady Melbourne, was mother-in-law to his lover, Caroline Lamb. Byron carried Caroline's pubic hair in a box and when his best friends left town, lapsed into depression and blamed the waters.

Marie-Therese, the daughter of Louis XVI and Marie-Antoinette, came here with her brothers Louis and Charles, later kings of France in a restored Bourbon monarchy. Marie-Therese was said to keep her father's bloodstained shirt with her.

Pittville

The Rotunda, Montpellier Spa Papworth's dome is derivitive of John Soane's Bank of England.

After Waterloo, Arthur, Duke of Wellington came to town at the height of Wellington-mania. The duke and duchess took the floor at a celebratory ball for 1,800 at the new, and hugely expensive, Assembly Rooms (now Lloyds Bank at Rodney Street).

To Bath's horror, Cheltenham became the Duke's spa of choice and with such an endorsement the spa took flight in the post-war years. The street traders were shooed from the High Street and given a covered market through a fancy oriental arch on Bennington Street. Development spread from the High Street to the Suffolks and Cambray. Sherbourne Spa opened in 1818. Henry

Thompson's son Pearson, hired John Papworth to enlarge the Montpellier Spa. Papworth, who later affected the name Buonarotti, created the Rotunda based on Villa la Rotunda, Vicenza, for Thompson's revamped baths. Montepellier Gardens were laid out with a Chinese pagoda for the band, steam-powered fountains and exotic glasshouses. With a dash of daring, ladies were allowed to dress down for Montpellier's soiree musicale and nearly 2,000 people attended the first event. Pearson had cleverly upstaged Kelly's Assembly Rooms.

In 1825 there was a seasonal company of 15,000 and a population of 20,000, 'Half clown and half cockney' said Cobbett, a resort 'of the lame and lazy, the gourmandising and guzzling.'

And so to Pitt whose imaginings devised a new town of 600 houses, gardens and lakes and a fabulous, temple-like pump room. Plots would be sold only to suitably professional buyers (including librarians, nurserymen and florists) obliged to build in a certain way: gothic and stuccoed and worth no less than £700. No servants would be allowed in the gardens save for nannies with children; there was no subletting of stables and yards and no boring for water.

A local man, John Forbes, was appointed architect and the design of the estate and the pump room are his, although the houses changed over the years it took to build them. In 1835 Forbes went to prison for fiddling his butcher. Compared to Pitt, he got off lightly.

In 1825, with only a few plots sold but the gardens laid and the pump house complete, the Bank of England imploded and the stock market crashed in a Barings-esque fable of greed and imaginings. A Scottish fantasist and adventurer, Gregor MacGregor, persuaded investors to risk huge sums in mineral-rich Poyais – a South American colony that existed only in MacGregor's head. Banks crashed and in the panic Pittville stuttered and limped. Pearson Thompson unloaded his part-finished Montpellier and Lansdown estates on the Jearrad brothers who sacked Papworth, the architect, but used his plans.

Pitt didn't go to the grand opening of the Pump Room in 1830. Perhaps he was sick of it. He'd poured money into the estate and still it wasn't enough. Wrong place, wrong time. The bright young things and super rich were looking for a new place to play and the seaside and the continental spas were now their thing. Besides, science was outrunning the spa doctors and the water was no longer a universal cure. A year before the Pump Room, the Imperial Spa was demolished. Ten years later, the Old Well buildings came down. By then Pitt's temple was a white elephant and he died with a half-finished vision and debts of half a million pounds.

In 1831 Thomas Billings began work on the Park. On Victoria's coronation day in 1838 he opened a zoo (Regent's Park had just opened) and showed two golden eagles, some monkeys and a Norwegian wolf. The company issued 4,000 £5 shares but the zoo flopped and was turned into a park with a lake and gardens. In 1839, Billings sold the site to Samuel Daukes who built the villas, including one for himself.

Temperance

In 1839 the Grand Temperance Festival hired the Pitville Pump Room for a tea party and but for a few 'votaries of Bacchus' (who went to a pub on the High Street) filled it to bursting point. Times were changing. Victoria was on the throne: virtue and a new morality were in vogue. TB, the 'White Plague', was endemic in London and the wealthy took to the coast for clean air and a restorative climate. That summer in Cheltenham more than 600 houses lay empty. With a population of 40,000 the town, like Bath, was overbuilt. To survive it needed to abandon the fiction of the spa and find a new metier as a place to live. It also needed to stop building houses and for the following forty years the town built only churches and schools, until the Winter Gardens in 1878 and the New Theatre (now the Everyman) in 1891.

As a jaded but gentle resort with advantages of climate and of class (after all, the gentry still kept houses here) Cheltenham appealed to the half-pay and retired veterans of the French Wars and the Punjab. The town was warm, clubbish and cheap, housing (and servants) were plentiful and a man returning from overseas could find a kindred spirit here.

Ex-servicemen and their families flocked here so that it was 'impossible to fire a shotgun and not hit a colonel or two'. Major Agg of the Hewletts came and, with a 'handsome independence in the Bengal Corps', built a grand house; Sherwood and Ingledew built houses in the Suffolks but most came with just a service pension and found they liked it well enough. They hunted with the Berkeley Hounds, played cricket and croquet and once or twice a year lost money at the races.

The army and navy needed to educate its sons and daughters: a decent education and one for which a man of modest means could pay. The 'Grammar and other Liberal Arts' school endowed by Pate in the sixteenth century was, as ever, in a row over trust money and on the brink of collapse. So, with Major-General George Swiney of the Royal Bengal Artillery presiding, a group of parents agreed to issue private shares in a new school. The money raised was enough to lease two houses in Bayshill and employ a small staff. Cheltenham College was never intended to be exclusively for service families and yet it has served the country well: 14 Cheltonians have won Victoria Crosses including Duncan Boyes, a 17-year-old midshipman.

In *Old Land Dog*, John Betjeman pokes fun at a 1950s Cheltenham almost wholly sustained by military families:

> Here's to General Artichoke
> the purplest man on earth
> Give three loud cheers for Cheltenham,
> the city of his birth.

In 1853, a Ladies College 'for the daughters and young children of Noblemen and Gentlemen' was established at Cambray House and in 1873, with Dorethea Beale as principal, moved to Bayshill. From her 'throne' above the organ in the Great Hall, Miss Beale prepared her girls to be the daughters of Empire. She taught them science and astronomy and when parents complained called it 'natural geography'. When she couldn't find teachers of the right calibre, she taught her own girls to teach and founded St Hilda's College, Oxford. She built the Arts and Craft Princess Hall 'to quicken the senses and stir the soul' (sadly, rupturing the old Well Walk

All Saints

Glass by Edward Burne-Jones and William Morris and beautiful arcades of polished granite where the figures seem in awe of their surroundings and ponder their faith and good luck. The screen is by William Letheren who had two wives and 22 children and was our greatest metalworker.

Synagogue, Synagogue Lane
A simple and discrete beauty for a congregation unsure of its tenure in a town torn by religious tensions.

that George III so loved) and adorned college with famous female exemplars.

The new, prim and sensible Cheltenham had done so much to sink the old that (an 1860 guide could say) the 'spread of education and intelligence' has 'done its work for good' and the 'gross or vicious habits of a past generation have fled or died out.'

Something had gone horribly right since the music stopped.

In fact, the town was gripped by evangelism and more especially, by one of its most ardent disciples: Francis Close. Close came to St Mary's in 1826 and was incumbent for 30 years. When Close preached his pulpit quaked with moral indignation. Colonel Berkeley and his race meetings merited special attention: Close raged against the 'vice and vicious excess' of the races which every year filled the town with the reckless and the brave. In his sermon – the 'Evil Consequences of attending the racecourse' – Close portrayed the colonel as the arch-libertine and even raised a crowd to remonstrate with the punters.

When the Chartist John Frost addressed 3,000 of the town's workers Close railed against socialists. 'It is impossible,' he told the Working Men's Association, 'for a minister to open his mouth without being conservative.'

Tennyson loathed him and called him 'pope' – an especially provocative sobriquet as Close despised Catholics – and at his house in St James Square wrote *In Memorium*:

> There lives more faith in honest doubt, believe
> me, than in half the creeds.

Honest or not, the 'potent vicar' had no doubts about his mission and used muscular Christianity to raise

donations for the first infants' schools and St Paul's teacher training college, now part of the University of Gloucestershire. The Evangelist Hannah Moore thought children should learn to read but not write, however, Close's schools taught both.

With the energy that built the spas and ballrooms, Cheltenham now built churches. Close built Holy Trinity as overflow for the parish church. Pearson Thompson gave land for Christ Church, designed by the Jearrads and consecrated in 1840. A pew at Christ Church was a measure of status and of income. St Paul's was a free church designed by John Forbes (architect of the Pump Room) for a growing working-class population. St Peter's was built on the Tewekesbury Road but few went to worship there. St Luke's was built for the college. Baptists, Wesleyans, Unitarians and Methodists, Quakers, Jews and even Catholics (many French exiles of the Napoleonic Wars) built their temples here. Catholic St Gregory's towers over the Bethal Chapel on Knapp Road, every inch antagonistic to the Evangelicals who tried to burn it down in 1850. Nearby, the Levis and the Issacs hid their synagogue off St James Square.

The churches and schools were built to save and to enlighten but not to empower the poor. The political machinery of the town – indivisible from its religion – turned in the same narrow space. The armchair colonels at the New Club thought the town a peaceful place for 'unprotected ladies' to 'walk about and enjoy themselves with the greatest freedom.' Who needs an elected corporation? Who needs a town hall or a free library that the poor might use? When Tory MP Agg-Gardiner petitioned for incorporation as a town with elected members and a mayor, the old guard – whose self-interest in the town's doings had turned corruption into high art – took their case to the Privy Council. They

Christ Church, Malvern Road

'A Staffordshire ornament that could stand on the largest chimneypiece in the world … a tower with an expression so lamentable you expect it to weep.' Harry Goodhart-Rendel

Those who did not have pews could buy tickets for services at a shilling a time, 1*s*. 6*d*. a day. To discourage sales at the church door, worshippers were encouraged to buy in advance. On the walls are memorials to officers of the Indian Army who died in the Punjab, Afghanistan and in Cheltenham. After years of poor time-keeping the clock was made to run accurately in 1996: 19 ticks and 19 tocks every minute.

lost. In 1876, Cheltenham became a town with a crest of pecking pigeons: *salubritas et eruditio*.

The conceit of the waters in the crest remained with the town. The Corporation bought the Pump Room and from time to time flogged the idea of a revival. 'Health comes happily at British Spas' said the adverts in the 1930s but in truth the game was up. The Edwardian town hall (a ballroom, not a municipal office) had fancy taps and nurses to dispense the water. The Pump Room attracted (and still attracts) curious tourists who drank the water and wished they hadn't. But nobody came for the cure. The last great gesture of the age was the Winter Gardens in Imperial Square, and they were demolished in 1938. In 1900, the Assembly Rooms were flattened and replaced by Lloyds Bank. The council built a library and a gallery to house Baron de Ferriere's gift of pictures and later a museum that will soon be replaced. Against the tide, in 1891, the Theatre Royal opened with Lily Langtry claiming 'With us returns at last – a golden age.'

Not quite a golden age, but perhaps a silver one.

Maturity

No more a libertine's playground or a cure, at least the Edwardian town could fill a beautiful theatre and a ballroom at the town hall, and play a cricket tournament in summer. It gave its young people to the First World War (600 College boys died) and its young people and its wrought-iron railings to the Second. Some ironwork has not yet been replaced and some is new, such as at Montpellier Gardens.

The spa has gone and save for one, the railway stations. The mineral water still flows but now visitors come to gaze at the beauty built around its foul taste, and for the music, science and literature festivals that fill the season. They come to gamble on the races and drown their sorrows in the hotel bars. There is knock-about jazz in the parks and old pop-stars at the Town Hall. Cheltenham even learned to build aeroplane parts and spy on enemies from GCHQ.

Like all English towns it was mucked about in the 1960s and 70s. Dozens of villas were lost or vandalised and gardens turned into car parks. It even got a skyscraper for Montpellier – a surrealist misfit. A ring road spoiled everything it touched. However, and perhaps it's more by luck than by judgement, the best of the Regency town remains and is gorgeous.

Montpellier is for window-shopping. At one end of the High Street there are shops that sell fruit and groceries and, at the other, haute couture and jewellery. On the narrow streets behind, where the fields once spread, there are tucked-away cafes and pubs with a sense of belonging.

The parks are for picnics, kick-arounds and pushchairs, for dog-walkers in the early morning and sleepers on a Sunday afternoon.

There where the long street roars hath been
The silence of the central sea (Tennyson)

Cheltenham is not breathtaking – there are no great vistas here – and yet there is hardly a better place to simply be, to read the paper on a bench and watch the world go by. It's a town in which to idly walk or, if you're with someone and feeling fancy, to promenade.

The Town

The High Street is the heart of the town, a market-place where shops have replaced stalls and where, at the western end, old alleys lead to streets of houses and chapels. At the east end you'll find the remnants of Cambray Mill and a leet, where water from the Chelt once turned the millstones.

Walk the High Street from east to west and the voices change, from refined Radio 4 to a good Gloucestershire burr. Here too, you'll hear languages from overseas. To the north, Winchcombe Street and Albion Street are knocked about but there are gems here, including a pseudo-Egyptian Masonic Hall. In Clarence Street the library and art gallery are out-gunned by an electricity substation.

Everyman Theatre opposite
Designer Frank Matcham's exuberant auditorium.
He also designed Blackpool Grand, Buxton Opera
House, the Grand Opera House Belfast, the London
Palladium and Hackney Empire.

Musical nymph, Imperial Circus above right

41

Well Walk left
A remnant of the original passage
from the parish church to
Skillicorne's well in Bayshill.

Cinema, Winchcombe Street above
Once the site of Highbury Congregational
Church and now an empty Art Deco Odeon.
On the facade pert maidens cavort with reels of
film. What would Francis Close have said?

Masonic Hall, Portland Street

From the street, the Egyptian-style hall with its
canted walls and masonic symbols in the
stonework, hints at what's to come. Inside, it's
pure 1820s Masonry.

The dining room is dressed as a Knights Templar
encampment, with a painted shield on the wall
behind each chair. Originally the ceiling was
painted to be a tent-like canopy but after-dinner
cigars soon obliterated it. The lodge room (no, it's
not a 'temple') has a sunburst, starry ceiling,
throne-like chairs on a typically Masonic
chequerboard floor and an organ in the gallery
held up by two pillars, each with a globe – one
celestial, one terrestrial – to symbolise Masonry
Universal. The building was finished in 1832 and
little has changed.

Regent Street above

Rodney Road
above right
Yellow for an old dowager: Swea Swedish restaurant and Jon's Hair Fashions.

High Street, east end
right
From timber-framed farm houses to Edwardian baroque and modern day pastiche, the High Street has evolved over centuries and, thoroughly commercialised, still rambles along its great west to east axis. It has been at the heart of the town for at least 600 years.

The Promenade at the High Street right
Edwardian baroque for the crossroads of
the town.

Royal Crescent left
For a town with grand pretensions, a
crescent. This one – Pitt's first venture –
was designed as two halves divided by a
carriageway. Instead it has a short,
single curve. In the post-French-War
depression a hungry mob broke the
door knockers. Edward Shewell lived
here with 16 children one of whom died
in the Charge of the Light Brigade with,
it's said, an open bible on his lap;
Shewell built the first waterworks at
Mythe (it flooded in 2007 leaving tracts
of the county without drinking water).
Princess Victoria visited number 18.

Gardner's Original Cheltenham Ale and Porter Brewery, Henrietta Street

Gardner began brewing in 1760. The company was bought by Whitbreads in 1963 and closed in 1998. Now it's a branch of Habitat, left, and a new shopping centre, above, where 'you can watch a movie, work out and enjoy great food' (at faux-American chain restaurants).

In best Cheltenham tradition, Henrietta Street has lovely ironwork, right.

**Theme and Variations,
Clarence Street**
Sculptor Barbara
Hepworth's modernist
bronzes are beautifully
at one with the old
Cheltenham & Gloucester
Building Society HQ.
Theme and Variations was
made between 1969 and
1972. Hepworth once said:
'I always know from the
beginning what a work is
going to look like.'

Alma House, Rodney Road

Even the names are redolent of Empire and the Union Flag still flies above Admiral Watts' opulent mansion. From Navy to Army, a succession of colonels and then a dairy company, now a mad mix of art nouveau and classical architecture and home to *This England* magazine.

Everyman Theatre, Regent Street

The New Theatre and Opera House opened in 1891 with a
production of *Lady Clancarty* (*Wedded and Wooed*) – a
romping Jacobite plot to assassinate William of Orange –
starring Lily Langtry with a 'bed chamber scene' in the
third act. Charlie Chaplin played here.

From the street there is no hint of the magic inside.

Public Library, Clarence Street

'People have too much knowledge already: it was
much easier to manage them twenty years ago.'
So said the *Looker On* in response to MP William
Ewart's Public Libraries Act. The free library was the
subject of bitter debate before it opened, in 1889, with
a carriage procession, cyclists, flags, hymns and church
bells. Now, behind its Edwardian facade, computers
provide unimagined access to information.

Electricity substation, Clarence Street
In 1895 Florence's Strozzi Palace came to Cheltenham in a
building which shows there was pride as well as power
generated by the town's first electricity supply.

Edward Wilson, The Promenade

'Words must always fail me when I talk of
Bill Wilson. I believe he really is the finest
character I ever met.'

Captain Robert Scott

In a cold evening light Kathleen Scott's statue of
Wilson is all angular strength and determination.
Wilson was born in Montpellier Parade and
became a doctor like his father, practising in the
east end of London. He was one of five men who
reached the South Pole on 17 January 1912 only to
find Amundsen's Norwegian flag already flying
there. All five died on the return journey.

Harward's Buildings opposite

From the High Street, Harward's Buildings are an
awesome introduction to the Regency Spa 'built
after the fashion of the Louvre.' Samuel Harward
was a bookseller and printer. The site was once
Lord's Meadow, mentioned in Domesday. Built as
private houses, they are now municipal offices.

The Promenade

Once a subscription only 'ride' from the High
Street to the Imperial (or Sherbourne) Spa
(now Queen's Hotel) and still the heart of
fashionable Cheltenham. 'No servant of any
description is allowed on the walk during the
hours of the promenade,' stated the Subscriber
rulebook. The top end is exactly twice as wide
as the lower end, a clever trick that makes it
seem longer than it really is.

The Promenade

'A verdant tunnel half a mile long', according to Rowe's 1845 *Guide*, and the most evocative of all Cheltenham streets – a reminder of the landscaped well walks and Regency opulence.

Trafalgar Street

Montpellier

At the end of the Promenade, Montpellier Walk was once the approach to Henry Thompson's spa with its Italianate rotunda. When the spa began to fade, Thompson's trees were cut down and replaced by shops propped up by sexy caryatids. Two of them were sculpted in London and the rest were copied locally, including two in 1970. On a warm summer morning Montpellier is best for coffee and newspapers at a pavement cafe.

Montpellier Gardens were once exclusively for spa-goers. During the First World War potatoes and cabbages grew here and young recruits drilled and marched along the paths. Imperial Gardens were once the walks for Imperial Spa and later home to the Winter Gardens. Now, the Town Hall pushes its backside into the space and artists sell their paintings here.

The Rotunda, Montpellier Street and **Montpellier Walk**
The dome of the Rotunda rises above the shops (far left). The summer balls were held here with 'delightful sets of quadrilles and waltzes'. Ladies were allowed to wear promenade dress but gentlemen wore formal. When the spa began to fail, the 'Walk' was replaced by shops and the street was laid out.

The chemist shop (above) on Rotunda Terrace was once the workshop of John Maskeleyne, magician and inventor of the ticket punch and coin-operated lock.

The Gordon Lamp

The lamp was raised by public subscription two years after Major-General Charles Gordon's defeat at Khartoum by 'Mad' Mahdi Muhammad Ahmad, in 1885.

The public, however, was not keen to remember Gordon's defeat and the town didn't want to pay for the gas. The project stumbled along for 30-odd years. An explanatory plaque was only added in 1934.

Montpellier Gardens

Unlike Bath, Cheltenham Spa had space to walk in and air to breathe. Then, as now, its gardens are an essential part of the Cheltenham experience.

Montpellier Arcade far left

Sussex Place above

Montpellier Street left

Gustav Holst, Imperial Square

A moon for Gustav Holst. It's by Anthony Stones, the Glossop-born sculptor who also did James Cook at the Maritime Museum in Greenwich. Stones has made Holst small and determined.

Queen's Hotel, Imperial Square

Walk towards the Queen's Hotel from the Promenade and see how it grows above the trees to become a massive Roman temple – the Temple of Jupiter in fact, upon which the Jearrad brothers' design is based. Cheltenham's grandest hotel was built in 1838 on the site of the Imperial Spa when the water dried up. Arthur Conan Doyle and Edward Elgar stayed, and Bob Hope played to American forces here.

Trafalgar Street left
Broadwalk right
Modern and faux-Regency housing around Imperial Square. The Broadwalk terrace was completed in 1998 – settling 200 years of indecision and showing that if you must copy something, copy it well. I had no idea it was faux but I should have guessed – where are the chimneys?

Tucked away at one end is Napoleon's Fountain, below, looted in Italy by the French, captured by British forces and sold to Thomas Henney, a Cheltenham solicitor and developer of the Sherbourne Spa.

Oriel Place above
Fancy work from 1826.

Imperial Square above left
The ironwork is archetypically Cheltenham.

Claremont Lodge left
Once home to Lady Combermere and, from 1919
to 1927, Dr James Shaw, who practised psychology at
St Bartholomew's in London. Shaw thought that by
playing sport, a woman would 'mar the beauty of her
face, change her nature and alienate male sympathy'.

Montpelier Spa Road right
From Claremont Lodge.

The Town Hall
Built to replace the Assembly Rooms (now Lloyds Bank)
the Town Hall opened in 1903 and hosts dances, concerts
and comics. Eddy Grant was here in a suit – so even
reggae singers dress up for its Edwardian opulence.

The Town Hall

The architect, Fred Waller of Gloucester, designed something for a city street, not the corner of a town park. The finished building was opened in December 1903 by Michael Hicks Beach who, as Chancellor of the Exchequer, habitually raised income tax every year to pay for war in South Africa. He is not commemorated in Britain but, strangely, Beachport, South Australia, is named after him. There was once spa water dispensed here but, ironically, health and safety assesors deemed the Doulton ware dispensers (right) a risk to drinkers and the taps are now dry.

Eagle Star Tower

Wherever you are, whatever the weather, the 161-foot, 13-storey octagon of Eagle Star Tower presides over the town's skyline. Since it was built in 1968 other crimes – like the out-of-town shopping at Kingsditch – have made it seem benign, but who would mourn its demolition? At least we could keep the brilliant, bad-tempered eagle.

Bath Road *and* beyond

Gothic splendours at Cheltenham College

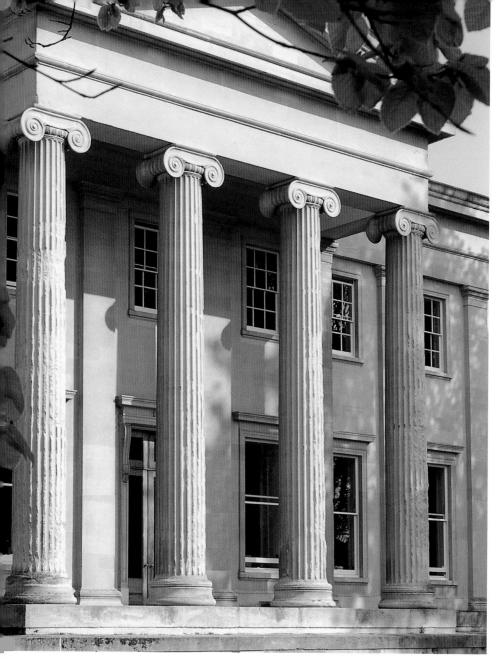

Cheltenham College Chapel right
The College once offered education for Military and Classical scholars. The old distinction is long gone but its memory survives in the chapel, built by local craftsmen in 1896: left for Military, right for Classics. The uncountable names of old boys killed in action in France and the Empire are desperately sad and reminded me of Kipling's *Arithmetic on the Frontier*:

A scrimmage in a border station
A canter down some dark defile
Two thousand pounds of education
Drops to a ten-rupee jezail

Thirlstaine House, Bath Road
When John Rushout, Lord Northwick, bought the house he added two wings for his paintings – 1,500 of them. Northwick was a great friend of Nelson and of William and Emma Hamilton. He owned property in Cheltenham and was the landlord of Anthony Trollope's father in Harrow, who fled to Belgium when the rent was overdue. After Northwick, the 'vello-maniac' Sir Thomas Phillips bought the house for his library of 160,000 books, to which he added 40 to 50 a week. In his will Phillips decreed that the collection should stay at Thirlstaine House and that no bookseller or stranger should rearrange them and that no Roman Catholic should view them. When the will failed, his grandson spent 50 years selling the collection. Today the boys and girls of Cheltenham College play music and study art here.

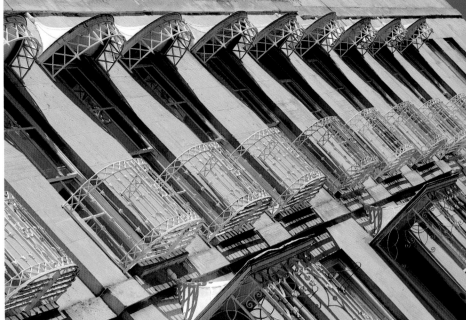

Oxford Parade, London Road

'The verandas and rails are composed of paper, silk and netting'. A description of the ironwork by Richard Marshall, a Sussex man who perfected his skills in Cheltenham and stayed here. Scenes from the BBC's 1995 adaptation of *Pride and Prejudice* were filmed on Oxford Parade.

Bath Road

Circular pods for new apartments behind Bath Road.

Sandford Park Lido

On a hot summer's day the Lido is the only place to be. There's a 50-metre pool, a children's pool and an old-fashioned cafe. The water is heated to 70 degrees so you don't have to be brave.

The Lido opened in 1935 with a swimsuit procession of the town's lovelies one of whom returned for a grand reopening in 2007.

Suffolks *and* Park

An immense Greek Revival terrace, friendly pubs, narrow streets and quirky local shops: the Suffolks is the community that town planners dream about.

The circular Park was planned as a zoo by Thomas Billings, who took a chance in a time of economic flux and lost. Samuel Daukes bought the company and built the villas that remain. Now, instead of monkeys there is a university in the middle.

The Beehive, Montpellier Villas John Forbes designed the Beehive when he was working on Pittville and lived down the road at number 31. Look for the aphorism around the beehive. A careless signwriter should have checked the spelling of Montpellier.
The Five Alls, Bath Road King, priest, judge, soldier and farmer for a pub sign.
The Corner Shop, Bath Road

Great Norwood Street
'We doctor your shoes, heel them
Attend to their dying and save their souls'

Around the Bath Road

A mosaic wall for the Indus Indian Restaurant, above.

Suffolk Square left
The immense asymmetry of the square was begun in 1823 by James Fisher who owned the Clarence Hotel (now John Dower House) and employed Edward Jenkins as architect. The north side, left, was finished 25 years later. Fisher gave land for the church (St James's) that is now a restuarant.

Suffolk Square right
Classical Greek columns and St James's.

Cheltenham Bowling Club below right
The club has been here since 1918, it's two greens hidden by high hedges. On a busy match night the best players demonstrate technique and nerve in a beautiful place.

The Park

The last of the five great estates to be laid out. The best of the eighteenth-century mansions are by Samuel Daukes who lived at Tudor Lodge, now demolished.

Tivoli Road left The actor Ralph Richardson was born here, at number 11.

Elwes Building, Park Campus above and right
A seafront pavillion? No, but a 'breezy seaside' building of light and space by Percy Thomas Partnership for the School of Business. Henry Elwes was Lord-Lieutenant of Gloucestershire who steered the old Cheltenham and Gloucester College to university status.

Tivoli Street, Alexandra Street and **Hatherley Street** opposite
A Saturday morning in summer and only a bicycle pump disturbs the air.

Bayshill *and* Lansdown

Bayshill is where the spa began, where William Mason found chalybeate water which his son-in-law, Skillicorne, commercialised.

Once farming land was freed from common use by the Enclosure Act, Bayshill was sold as plots for development and building began.

Here, Regency Cheltenham entertained a king at Fauconberg House (now gone) and built the best villas outside of London.

Henry Thompson's grand plans for Lansdown faltered in an economic crash. His son Pearson sold up to the Jearrads who helped themselves to much of Papworth's original designs.

Queen's Parade

This terrace started badly when the financial crash interrupted building work in the 1830s, but who could forsee it would only be finished 150 years later? One end is old and the other new, but only local knowledge or sharp light reveals which is which. Arthur 'Bomber' Harris was born at number 3. The morality of his 'thousand bomber' raids on German cities (and especially Dresden) is still debated.

Bayshill Road

'Bayshill Road is one of the great roads for architecture in all England.'
David Verey, Pevsner's *Gloucestershire*

The Skillicornes sold this land in 1837 and by 1843 it had become '2 handsome rows of houses and also a number of detached villas … several of which are occupied by resident families of affluence and station'.
Henry Davies

Cheltenham Ladies' College

'A ladies' college has just sprung up here and . . . every judicious person sees many evils arising from it.' Elizabeth Holmes, 1874

The Ladies' College will forever be associated with Dorothea Beale, educational pioneeer, campaigner for women's rights and founder of St Hilda's College, Oxford. Appointed principal at just 27, Miss Beale reigned for 50 years. Her *gels* would learn to be doctors and scientists, artists and geographers – *and* they played hockey. To appease parents science was called 'natural geography'.

Later in life Miss Beale bought a tricycle and each morning was pushed up Bayshill to freewheel down. She is remembered with her fellow-educationalist Frances Mary Buss in the ryhme:

> Miss Buss and Miss Beale, Cupid's darts do not feel.
> How different from us, Miss Beale and Miss Buss.

Miss Beale would approve of today's confident, outgoing girls, the arts building and the newly-renovated observatory on the top of the tower. She might not like the backpacks.

Princess Hall, Cheltenham Ladies' College

On this site in 1718, William Mason put a fence around a spring of water. Later, his son-in-law Henry Skillicorne built a beautiful Corinthian ballroom here and the spa was born.

None of which survived Miss Beale's zeal. The school's move to the present site ruptured the old Well Walk that George III so loved. Then, in 1895 Miss Beale commissioned the Arts and Crafts Princess Hall 'to quicken the senses and stir the soul'. It was one of the first public buildings in Cheltenham to have electric light.

The wooden columns look almost too delicate to support the tiers and an organ but, in a clever trick, hidden in the wood is a steel frame. Around the proscenium arch is J Eadie Reid's frieze, *A Dream of Fair Women*, a Pre-Raphelite fantasy of heroines real and mythical.

Royal Well Terrace above left
The George Hotel above
York Terrace far right
Little Bayshill Terrace right
Bayshill Road left

Lansdown Place above and right
Said to be 'One of the most cheerful of suburban situations . . . with extensive views of open country.'

Lansdown Parade
far right

Lypiatt Terrace
opposite
Built speculatively by local builder Richard Keightly in around 1848, probably advised by Painswick architect Charles Baker.

Lansdown Terrace
left and right
John Papworth's monumental vision was adopted by the Jearrads and took ten years to build. It was finished around 1835 and is now beautifully restored.

Lansdown Crescent right
The public face of the Jearrads' unusually convex terrace is no match for the back, where mews workshops and brightly-painted brick make up for the sunless outer curve.

Pittville *and* Prestbury

'We drove in a horse fly to visit Pittville in the suburbs of Cheltenham, a scene of gorgeous magnificence. Here a large estate has been divided into public gardens, and sprinkled with houses of every size, shape and character: Grecian temples, Italian villas, and citizen's boxes, so fresh and clean, you would imagine they were all blown out at once like soap bubbles.'
Catherine Sinclair, 1833

Albert Road
'It is curious to see the names that the vermin owners have put upon their houses here.'
William Cobbett

Dorset Villa, Pittville Lawn
A Greek Christmas cake for Pittville: the most
extravagant villa on the estate and almost
certainly by estate architect John Forbes.

Wellington Square, **Clarence Square** and **Pittville Lawn** clockwise from above
Pitt's sniffy insistence on stucco mansions interspersed with terraces for his
new town was lost in financial mayhem and years of empty or half-finished
plots. The later, stone-faced houses of Clarence Square bring a touch of
Victorian gothic to the neighbourhood.

Pittville Pump Room

In a low winter sun the Pump Room glows magically. Pitt didn't go to the grand opening of his apotheosis and later died hopelessly in debt. The architect, Forbes, went to prison for cheating his butcher. The statues are Aesculapius the Greek god of medicine, above, Hygeia (health) and Hippocrates (the physician).

Pittville Pump Room left and above
A playground for William Cobbett's 'tax-eaters' – 'the lame and lazy, the gourmandising and guzzling' to while away their time. But too late – already the fashion for taking the waters was waning when the Pump Room opened in 1830. Now, Cheltenham's greatest expression of Regency manners is a venue for concerts and weddings.

The 1825 pump and bore hole right
The entire success of the Pump Room depended on a flow of iron-rich water supplied by this now redundant pump – hidden from sight beneath the grand architecture overhead.

4 Clarence Road

The Regency drawing room precedes Gustav Holst's birth here, in 1874, and is probably the only truly Regency interior in town.

Jupiter, the bringer of Jollity is at the piano. Apparently Holst chose this instrument (and paid £12 for it) for its light touch – he suffered neuritis in his right arm and couldn't practice without pain.

Gustav's younger brother Emil ran away to London to be an actor (their father, a pianist, disapproved) and after the First World War went to Hollywood. There, he played alongside Noel Coward, Humphrey Bogart and, in *John loves Mary*, Ronald Reagan.

The *Planets* suite was influenced by Holst's interest in astrology, rather than astronomy, and so there is no *Earth*.

The house is now a museum.

Prestbury Racecourse

A punter contemplates the 'Evil Consequences of attending the racecourse', home of Francis Close's 'vice and vicious excess'.

Index